Educate US?
All translated.

Straddien cultures

Influence of Chinese Trad

Of Flesh & Spirit

# of flesh & spirit

POEMS BY WANG PING

COFFEE HOUSE PRESS

MINNEAPOLIS

Some of the poems have appeared in the following magazines and anthologies: *The Best American Poetry 1993* and *1996, The Chicago Review, Critical Quarterly, The Literary Review, The Portable Lower Eastside, River City, Sulfur, Talisman, West Coast Line,* and *The World.*

This book is made possible in part by support from National Foundation for the Arts and New York Foundation for the Arts.

Coffee House Press is supported in part by a grant provided by the Minnesota State Arts Board, through an appropriation by the Minnesota State Legislature, and in part by a grant from the National Endowment for the Arts. Significant support has also been provided by The McKnight Foundation; Lannan Foundation; Jerome Foundation; Target Stores, Dayton's, and Mervyn's by the Dayton Hudson Foundation; General Mills Foundation; The St. Paul Companies; Butler Family Foundation; Honeywell Foundation; Star Tribune/Cowles Media Company; James R. Thorpe Foundation; Dain Bosworth Foundation; Pentair, Inc.; Beverly J. and John A. Rollwagen Fund of the Minneapolis Foundation; the law firm of Schwegman, Lundberg, Woessner & Kluth, P.A.; the Helen L. Kuehn Fund of the Minneapolis Foundation; and many individual donors. To you and our many readers across the country, we send our thanks for your support.

Coffee House Press books are available to the trade through our primary distributor, Consortium Book Sales & Distribution, 1045 Westgate Drive, Saint Paul, MN 55114. For personal orders, catalogs, or other information, write to: Coffee House Press, 27 N. 4th Street, Suite 400, Minneapolis, MN 55401.

LIBRARY OF CONGRESS CIP DATA

Wang, Ping, 1957–

    Of flesh and spirit ; poems / by Wang Ping.

      p. cm.

    ISBN 1-56689-068-3 (pb : alk. paper)

    1. Title.

PS3573.A4769O37   1998   97-43-43199

811'.54—DC21   CIP

10 9 8 7 6 5 4 3 2 1

Contents

AUTHOR ACKNOWLEDGMENT: Special thanks to Lewis Warsh for his inspiration and unconditional support throughout the book. Also, thanks to the Poetry Project and Writer's Room for providing warm, encouraging environments. I'd also like to thank the following individuals for their support: Adam Lerner, Chuck Wachtel, Jocelyn Lieu, Ed Friedman, Bob Hershon, Donna Brook, Donna Brodie, Richard Sieburth, Anne Waldman, Arthur Sze, Lyn Hejinian, Cathy Bowman, Clayton and Caryl Eshleman, and Gil Mestler.

for Ariel and Haixia

Syntax

She walks to a table
She walk to table

She is walking to a table
She walk to table now

What difference does it make
What difference it make

In Nature, no completeness
No sentence really complete thought

Language, like woman
Look best when free, undressed

These Images

Thus like swans,
wings wide open in the air,
when spring splashes lakes onto shores,
where in the woods,
wild ducks wheeling in pairs
for a love nest, and snakes,
after spring's first thunders,
slide forth from winter's fields,
when raccoons lose their minds
mating among maple leaves
in Quaker cemeteries,
and golden smoke rises
above cypress trees, their needles
aquiver with too much pollen,
when songs flow from lips
and bare feet welcome the embrace of sand,
where, under the tent of a white sheet,
eyes fall on the sea-drenched forehead
of the beloved,
when the church bell rings,
children dash through the lunchroom,
their jackets of tropical fruit and birds of paradise
against the concrete ground of P.S. 19,
where words are at stake
and thoughts immobilized,

where life shouts with joy
and being is beauty and love
no longer clings,
where senses quicken their steps
to enter hearts of things . . .

So simple, these images,
their recognition
is in our nature,
yet too often neglected,
our eyes already elsewhere.
It is beyond the gods
why we hold onto our sorrows
so long, and so stubborn.

Of Flesh & Spirit

I was a virgin till twenty-three, then always had more than one lover at the same time—all secret.

In China, people go to jail for watching porno videos while condoms and pills are given out free.

When I saw the first bra my mom made for me, I screamed and ran out in shame.

For a thousand years, women's bound feet were the most beautiful and erotic objects for Chinese. Tits and asses were nothing compared to a pair of three-inch "golden lotuses." They must have been crazy or had problems with their noses. My grandma's feet, wrapped day and night in layers of bandages, smelled like rotten fish.

The asshole in Chinese: the eye of the fart.

A twenty-five-year-old single woman worries her parents. A twenty-eight-year-old single woman worries her friends and colleagues. A thirty-year-old single woman worries her bosses. A thirty-five-year-old woman is pitied and treated as a sexual pervert.

The most powerful curse: fuck your mother, fuck your grandmother, fuck your great-grandmother of eighteen generations.

One day, my father asked my mother if our young rooster was mature enough to jump, meaning to "mate." I cut in before my mother answered: "Yes, I saw him jump onto the roof of the chicken coop." I was ten years old.

Women call menstruation "the old ghost," science books call it "the moon period," and refined people say "the moonlight is flooding the ditch."

My first lover vowed to marry me in America after he took my virginity. He had two kids and an uneducated wife, and dared not ask the police for a divorce. He took me to see his American Chinese cousin who was staying in the Beijing Hotel and tried to persuade his cousin to sponsor him to come to New York. But his cousin sponsored me instead. That's how I'm here and why he went back to his wife, still cursing me.

Chinese peasants call their wives: that one in my house; old Chinese intellectuals: the doll in a golden house; in socialist China, husbands and wives call each other "my lover."

The story my grandma never tired of telling was about a man who was punished for his greed and had to walk around with a penis hanging from his forehead.

We don't say "fall in love," but "talk love."

When I left home, my father told me: "never talk love before you're twenty-five years old." I waited till twenty-three. Well, my first lover was a married coward. My first marriage lasted a week. My husband slept with me once, and I never saw him again.

Sparks

When I was eight
I lit a coal stove every morning
staring at the sparks jump and
dance out of flames
as I fanned them with a palm leaf
Mother said they were fairies in exile
turned into diamonds
She knit a crown
to adorn my childhood

When I was eight
I went fishing in a flooded stream
I floated on water
pebbles were my pillows
I looked up at the milky clouds
spreading across the sky
Father said they were angels in exile
turned into waterfalls
He folded a boat
to bear away my childhood

She Is That Reed

Don't point at your giggling daughter
and say: My last child, her name is Reed.

Don't stop your spinning wheel, your eyes at the pond,
"Why should girls be called flowers? I want to name her Reed."

Mother, oh my mother who called me Reed,
your story shocked me so much I swallowed an apricot pit.

"My last daughter couldn't cry when she was born.
Your aunt made a reed flute to call you back."

"Mouth to mouth, the flute brought your first cry.
Ain't I right that I named you Reed?"

"A good name," I said, but why was I giggling again?
You pulled my ear and said: "You are still Reed even though
    you learned how to read."

Mother, oh my mother who called me Reed,
Years passed, do you still remember that reed?

You held my hand and blew the flute hard,
your tears and sweat caught me back to your dark warm cave.

How ugly I was, mother, thin and stubborn like grass in the pond,
but you knew you'd never have to worry about me again.

We roamed around valleys to pick wild fruits and pigeon eggs,
and walked fifteen miles to sell them at the fair for my tuition.

I'm probably the only person on earth saved by a reed,
I blushed every time you told the story to a stranger.

"Only a crying baby could live and grow," you smiled,
"I like my daughter whirling around the Yellow Plateau like the wind."

I'm looking more and more like you, mother,
except my hair has grown beyond the river beyond the sea.

If you see a strange college girl walking down the valley,
she's that Reed, mother, who blasted out her first cry into your flute.

Flag Signal

When the March wind blew,
my birth put you at peace.
You lifted me to the window
to see spring pouring onto each tree.
"I'll make you a boat with purple sails," you said,
"to catch yellow bass in the peach blossom current."

In March you came home from the sea,
and pulled out the chessboard before taking off your boots.
You started well but always lost in the end.
In my triumphant uproar you kept silent.
Suddenly you pinched my nose till I cried.
Laughing, you picked me up on your shoulders
and walked out to see

March wind pushing the horizon,
waves upon waves
like flocks of sheep napping with their heads in their necks.
You pointed here and there, murmuring:
the sea and sky gaze and roar at each other—this is nature.
I played with your deformed half ear.
"Daddy, you can hear me talking without the hearing aid,
is it also nature?"

That year March was wet and muddy.
You carried my luggage to the farm.

I heard your sighs mingled with your breathing.

When I asked you to rest and wipe your sweat,

you gestured to me to listen

to the rhythm of migrating birds returning south,

the running of juice in old trees,

and the new branches growing in their own directions.

Before I could say good-bye,

you left and never looked back.

The day I brought you my first poem published in America,

your arms were attached to I.V. bottles.

I translated it word by word.

Finally you forgave my betrayal of your purple boat.

You were not disappointed that I didn't get rich from my poems.

You told me to pour the glass of cognac back into the bottle.

"No more drinking or smoking," you announced,

"I'm learning English to sail on the American Pacific

and pick magic herb among the Rocky Mountains."

Resurrection

Who said a soul can't cross the sea? Last night, you slipped through my door again (three Medicos plus a latch), like a raindrop drifting into a broken dream. You leaned on the red brick wall, unwinding the endless bandages on your feet.

surreal

Eighty years, all carved on your huge heels and toeless soles. Your lips squirmed with your last request: a banana and a black silk gown.

No need to apologize, Nainai, for your reproaches or spankings. I only remember your tears of joy for the first bite of ice cream on your 79th birthday. It was a Friday. We were standing outside a food store on the Nanjing Road when you suddenly said it was your birthday. And I said, "Oh, let's celebrate," and ran in to get you a chocolate ice cream brick.

Please do not look at me with those bleak eyes. Even father's filial piety couldn't stop mother's fury and keep you at home. The night I carried you on the ship for Qingdao, I dreamed of turning into surging waves to retrieve your fading steps. I didn't realize until then that my childhood had been a vine hanging over the precipice of your life.

Do not wave your bandages at me. My feet have grown as hard as white poplars in our native town. I'll make a pair of wings with them, to carry your soul into spring, into the forest and grass, into a world without memory. Be a bird, a bee, or even a fly. Just to live again, with joy.

Born in the Year of Chicken

On the first day of the year of chicken, my mother sent me a fortune card with a golden coin of a rooster glued on the back: "You'll have prosperity and fame in 1993." On the second day of the year of chicken, my sister sent me a card, warning me that I should wear a red string around my waist to avoid disasters.

One of my childhood diversions was to read the court posters. Among the penalties for rapists and murderers, I often saw "two-year imprisonment" for *ji jian*. The two characters— "chicken" and "fuck"—puzzled and fascinated me. Twenty years later, I met a college girl who had once participated in a trial for homosexuals. After I confessed my ignorance of the subject, she whispered mysteriously: "You're from the countryside. You must have seen how chickens mate." At this moment, the two characters—*ji jian*—rang a bell.

We don't say "trifles," but *ji mao suan pi*—chicken feathers and garlic skin.

When I was a peasant in the countryside, my best companions were a red hen and a brown duck. The hen would lay eggs only in my bed, and the duck loved to drink from my chamber pot in the morning.

A tip from the old Chinese sayings: Rise at cock-a-doodle-do and you'll stay healthy till one hundred and two.

On my birthday, my grandma always slipped a boiled egg dyed red into my hand and told me to eat it quickly behind the door so my sisters wouldn't get jealous.

I remember every spring, when an old man in a greasy gray jacket appeared in the New Ocean Navy Compound, all the families rushed to him with their young roosters. The man tied each frightened creature on long chopsticks, cut the side open and dug out two white eggs with a thin spoon. Then he filled the wound with the feathers he pulled from the screaming victim. The crowd watched silently with their mouths open in awe. No one would tell me what it was all about. I bugged my father until his ears buzzed. "Castration," he finally said, waving me away. "Why roosters only?" I chased him to his bedroom. "It's not fair." "Use your head," he roared. "Hens lay eggs. Roosters can do nothing except screw hens and crow their lungs out in the morning. Now get out."

A castrated rooster tastes better than a hen, especially if it's steamed or sautéed.

A recipe for mothers who can't produce milk: a hen (the older the better; best if it hasn't laid any eggs for three or four years) and five ounces of pangolin scales. Break the scales into small pieces and sew them into the stomach of the hen. Cook until the flesh comes off the bones. Eat the meat and drink the soup.

"Looking for bones in an egg" means "finding faults" or "starting a fight."

On holidays, my mother would pick out a chicken from the coop, usually a hen who was too old to lay eggs, and make soup. I couldn't eat the chicken I'd raised for years. But if I told the truth, my sisters would laugh at me for being a sentimental petty bourgeois. So I said I couldn't eat myself since I was born in the year of chicken. It wasn't really necessary.

My family was delighted that there was one less person to share the hen.

Sometimes I wonder why Chinese call crosseyes *dou ji yan*—gamecock's eyes, and corns on feet *ji yan*—cock eyes.

The literal meaning of *ji ba*—penis—is "chicken stick." Till I was 33, I thought it meant vagina. After long hours of meditation on why I'd made such an error, I decided it was my father's fault. He used to shout *ji ba* to my mother when he was angry, together with other curses alluding to women's private parts.

There's a book called *240 Ways of Eating Chickens.*

 I had a hen who loved to hatch. Every time she laid her tenth egg, she'd make a nest with grass and squat there with her feathers puffing out, not eating, not sleeping. My grandma tried various methods to wake her up so she would be productive again. She soaked the hen in icy and warm water by turns, stuffed food into her mouth, blindfolded her and hung her upside down on a tree. But she always managed to stagger back to her empty nest. On the twentieth day, she'd start laying eggs again. It was as regular as a woman's period. Finally my mother was fed up and made a pot of holiday soup with her.

I reported to my mother that I eat chicken legs and wings every day in New York. "How lucky you are!" she wrote back. "I've been working hard all my life and I can still only afford two or three chickens a year." My mother measures her living standard by counting how many chickens she has eaten that year: 3—poor; 5—so-so; 7—good; 10—rich. So every Christmas, I send her a card with this message: Dear mother, enclosed is a hundred dollars. Please buy yourself some chickens to strengthen your health.

During the Cultural Revolution, folk prescriptions spread and changed like fashions. At times everybody was eating vinegar eggs; every other family was brewing red bacterial tea. In the early seventies, people injected themselves with spring roosters' blood as tonic. During those years, my roosters were spared from castration; but they had to endure the blood transfusion once a week.

My lover's kids became vegetarians after they learned how Perdue chickens were raised.

The stinkiest thing on earth is the shit of a hatching hen.

Another tip from the Chinese sayings: A golden phoenix can fly out of a chicken coop.

When I was nine, I had a crush on an old peddler who traded malt sugar for old newspapers, used clothes, and chicken feathers. He was dirty and sickly. His head was bald and his tummy stuck out. Someone said he used his saliva to make his candy. But all this didn't matter. He was my first fantasy lover. I saved my best feathers and waited anxiously for his monthly arrival. I loved the way he chipped a piece of candy off his metal plate and placed it in my palm. If he had just given me a look and said: "Hey, kid, come with me," I'd have gone anywhere with him.

I told you I'm just a chicken. You laughed heartily and entered me from behind.

Female Marriage

Chinese characters for marriage: *qu* 娶—a man getting married, and *jia* 嫁—a woman getting married.

Jia 嫁 is made of two components: the left part is nü 女—woman, and the right part, *jia* 家—home.

If a thirty-year-old woman still remains single, every member of her family, every female colleague of hers, gets busy to find her a husband. If she shows no interest, she's suspected of being a hermaphrodite. But if she shows too much interest, or changes boyfriends constantly, she'll be called a "broken shoe," "rotten meat," or *zou ma deng*—lanterns with paper-cut figures made to revolve when it's lit, something like a dizzying merry-go-round.

Every Chinese believes that a husband is a woman's *guisu*—her final home to return to.

Nainai stands for paternal grandma. Its literal translation is "breast breast," or "milk milk."

Waipo stands for maternal grandma. *Wai* means "outside," "stranger." *Po,* "old woman."

My Waipo used to weep when she brushed my hair. "What are you going to do, my baby? Your hair is too tough, so will be your fate. Try not to be so pigheaded, try to learn some obedience. Otherwise you'll never find a husband."

Fu chang fu sui—when man sings, wife follows.

Nuzi wu cai bian shi de—ignorance is woman's virtue.

My father's favorite curse to my mother is *bi yang de*—born out of a cunt, as if he came out of something else.

Other curses for women:

    Cheap stuff

    Losing money commodity

    Disastrous flood

    Stinky whore

    Fox spirit

    Shrew

Even Confucius, the wisest and kindest saint, complained that women and inferior men are hard to raise.

For seventy-five years, my Nainai walked on her heels because all her toes were broken and bent under the soles to make a pair of "golden lotuses." She brought up her two sons alone, by working in the fields and delivering babies for her neighbors. I don't know her name. No one knows her name, not even herself. When she was a girl, she was called a girl, maybe Number 1 or Number 2. When she got married, her neighbors called her "wife of so-and-so," and her husband called her *wei*—equivalent to "hello." After she had her first son, she got the name "mother of so-and-so."

When I was a kid, I was crazy about keeping my hair long. But my father cursed at me every time he saw me brushing it, and my mother chased me around with a pair of scissors.

All our lives, we've never felt attractive enough.
But for whom do we struggle to look beautiful?

Chinese proverbs: A married daughter is spilt water. If she marries a chicken, she becomes a chicken; if she marries a dog, she becomes a dog.

Confucius says: "It is not pleasing to have to do with women or people of base condition. If you show them too much affection, they become too excited, and if you keep them at a distance, they are full of resentment.

Never deal with a businesswoman, Chinese men often warn each other. They are too powerful, well-armed with thousands of years of experiences in intrigues and plots to survive in family and society.

With a pair of "golden lotuses," she enters the code of "pure love," a code of tears and suffering.

Thanks to her small feet, my Nainai was able to get married even before her period started. She gave birth to two boys and a girl. When she was 25, her husband died. She was given two choices: marry again and leave her boys, her house and land to the care of her husband's relatives, or stay in her late husband's house as a widow forever and bring up the kids. She chose the second, not only because she couldn't bear separating from her boys, but also because her husband's early death had given her a bad name, and no decent man would go near her.

A woman with high cheek bones brings bad luck to her husband—a sign of "husband killer."

It's also bad luck for men to walk under a clothesline with women's underwear drying on it.

By becoming martyrs, we managed to leave some names for ourselves in the vast army of the anonymous: concubines, courtesans, a few empresses, a few poets and soldiers, the other half of the sky, and the girls of iron.

Yu gui—return home, standing for female marriage, first appeared in the "Book of Songs" about two thousand years ago. Girls are homeless until they get married, until they *chu jia*.

She called in the voice of a human. She called in the voice of a woman. But no one would help her out of the abyss. Only when she pretended to be her own child and report herself as a negligent mother did someone take her away in handcuffs to make her function as a mother again.

Some women cover their faces with veils and some with powder.

Old plus a female noun always makes a good insult: old woman, old girl, old cow, old bitch, old crone, old bat, old hag, old mother-in-law.

I asked my Nainai why she sold her daughter for a morsel of food. "To keep your father and uncle alive," she said. "You'd have done the same. If something happened to my boys, both my daughter and I would be thrown out of the house, and we'd both have died. Everything was under their names, no matter how young."

My sister was divorced for giving birth to a girl. She didn't blame her husband, or her mother-in-law who forced her son to choose another woman. She blamed only her failed womb which couldn't bear an heir for the family.

There are 223 characters with the component of *nü*— woman. Many of them show woman as the source of all misfortunes and evils:

Nu 奴 : slaves, the name women called themselves.

Bi 婢 : woman slave.

Jian 奸 : evil, traitor, and adultery (another way to write this word is to put three women on top of each other).

Ru 如 : follow, obey.

Ji 妓 : prostitute.

Yao 妖 : all the things that are alien, abnormal, monster, evil.

Du 妒 : jealousy. Other words for this meaning (all with woman as the component: ji, mao, jie).

Ping 姘 : adultery, a couple living together without a marriage certificate.

Lan 婪 : greedy.

Xian 嫌 : suspicion.

Lan 嬾 : lazy.

Piao 嫖 : go whoring.

Ask a Chinese man why women are associated with disasters, he'll immediately give you a list of those who ruined the greatest emperors and brought down entire kingdoms: Daji, a fox spirit; Yang Guifei, a fat concubine; Chen Yuanyuan, a prostitute.

I think of what happened to my grandmothers, what's happening to my mother and my sister, all those years of not knowing where or who they are. I'm not taking that road. But the only way for help is to think back through my grandmothers and my mother.

The national curse for Chinese is *ta ma de*—his mother's (cunt).

The most vicious curse for men is *jue zi jue sun*—May you have no son!

What Are You Still Angry About

I guess I should feel lucky.
I wasn't aborted as a fetus
or thrown into a chamber pot as a baby.
I no longer need to break my toes to make lotus feet
or squish my liver and kidneys to slim my waist.
I should feel lucky
that I'm not packed at the bottom of a rusty ship,
thinking I'm going to a free country,
but only end up jumping into the ocean,
or crouching in a detention center in Mexico
waiting to be processed.
Lucky I don't have to worry about being deported in plastic handcuffs
with brown spray in my hair.
Lucky I'm not locked in some moldy basement in Bay Ridge,
raped at night and working for minimum wage during the day.
Yes, I must feel lucky
that I have vocations other than love or maternity:
I'm a poet, a teacher, and working toward a Ph.D.

But I must be an ungrateful beast
because I always feel like screaming with my broken voice.
How can I explain the anger that prevents me from breathing?
I want to scream
every time I bow to my family tree which hangs in the clan hall.
It records the men of Wang family for over fifty generations

whereas the names of my female ancestors
just vanish like tadpole tails.
I scream, but I have no voice.
So I write this genealogy along maternal lines.

My mother was born in Shanghai in 1940. My grandpa Wai-gong, being an educated man, didn't mind at all that his first child was a girl. He gave her a beautiful name, Shen Laichun—"bring spring." (My two aunts didn't have that luck; they were named Laidi—"bring brother," and Zhaodi—"lure brother.") He even sent her to the best music school in Shanghai to become a pianist. But she ruined everything by eloping with a Navy officer to an island and had a baby at the age of seventeen. She didn't really like children, but my father wanted a son to pass down his family name, so she had three more babies until a boy was born. Gradually she became bitter, stuck on the island teaching music at a boring middle school. She had an affair with another Navy officer who promised to bring her back to Shanghai. But when he found out she could no longer have children, he left without a word. After her husband died, she quit her job and became a fortune teller and tai chi master, traveling around the country to heal the deaf and mute and those who can't be cured with normal medicine. At the age of fifty-three, she has become a famous sorceress.

P-tuo

Waipo, my seventy-three-year-old maternal grandma is called Chen Duoni. Duo means extra; ni, girl. She was the

33

second child of a poor peasant family in Jiangsu Province. The birth of her sister had already disappointed parents and grandparents, so the birth of Duoni was really unwelcome. Her five younger sisters were all drowned in the chamber pot by her paternal grandma. Duoni was very pretty, with thick black hair and long curly eyelashes. At thirteen, she was able to help her mother give birth to her eighth child. Her elder sister had married, and her grandma already passed away. When she cut the umbilical cord, her mother asked, "Duoni, a boy or a girl?" "A girl, mom," Duoni answered in a trembling voice. Her mother collapsed. "Child, put her in the chamber pot."

Duoni held the bloody baby in her arms. "I can't, mom, I can't!"

"Hand me the cheap stuff," the father roared from outside the door.

Duoni knelt down. "Please, mom and dad, let the baby live. Sell me so that you can raise my sister. Let her live at least to my age."

So Waipo sold herself to a textile factory in Shanghai as a *bao shenggong*—indentured laborer. She worked five years, fourteen hours a day, seven days a week, without pay or the freedom to go out. Still, she survived, and survived quite well. She was the most skillful worker in the factory. She liberated her lotus feet, which had been bound when she was seven. It was even more painful to straighten those broken bones, bent under the soles than to bind them in the first place. My Waipo had to soak her feet in urine for two hours every night—a folk prescription to soften the bones—before she tried to pull them back into their normal positions. When she was finally free at the age of eighteen, she declined a job offer from her factory, married my grandpa, a handsome clerk at an important Hong Kong bank, and became the mother of five children. My Waipo is the most intelligent and energetic woman I've ever seen. Without going to school, she learned how to read and write. She can repeat things people said ten, twenty, fifty years ago, with such authority that you can never ever doubt their authenticity. And she is always engaged in some project or scheme which often ends up with troubles and headaches. If she had been born in a right age, she could have been a great politician or a diplomat, at least an excellent spy.

Taiwaipo, my maternal great-grandma, was born in 1902. She was the first child, but was named Zhang Ernu—the second girl. Her parents hoped that the goddess of birth, hearing that this family already had two daughters, might feel sorry for them and send them a son as soon as possible. The trick worked. Two years later, Ernu's mother gave birth to a son. As the parents were grateful to Ernu for bringing an heir to the family, they allowed their daughter to live with them until she was seventeen. Usually a seventeen-year-old girl could get a much bigger betrothal, but Ernu was sold for only five silver yuan, a pot of wine and three bowls of pork noodles.

Her father, a gambling addict, had been searching for a husband for Ernu to get some cash to pay off his debts. His wife, a well-known shrew, managed to ruin all his deals. In his despair, he sold his wife for a hundred and fifty silver yuan and lost it all in the gambling den the same night. On his way home, he met Scholar Fan, an opium addict from the neighborhood. He had just married off his daughter the day before and was now on his way to the opium den. Ernu's father wanted a loan. Scholar Fan told him that he had only five yuan left after paying off his debt, and he needed a few puffs really badly; besides, experience had taught him never to lend money to a gambler. Ernu's father pulled him back and said he had a seventeen-year-old daughter, a perfect match for Fan's twenty-year-old son. So they went to a restaurant, drank a pot of rice wine, ate three bowls of noodles, and made a deal. The next day, Ernu left a gambler's house and entered a drug addict's family.

My great grandma gave birth to eight children, all girls. Three survived, and the rest were all drowned by her mother-in-law. Because she didn't bear a son to carry her husband's name, she felt inferior all her life, and never complained about his daily fists and insults. She believed that she must have done something horrible in her previous life, and was now being punished.

The mother of my great-grandma had two names, Zhang Ching Mei and Wu Hehua. When she was sold to the Wu family as a daughter-in-law-to-be at five, her mother-in-law changed her name from Ching Mei to Hehua, to claim both her body and soul, and she called her only by her son's name, "San Mao's so-and-so."

She also rebound the girl's feet. Hehua was known for her small lotus feet in her own village, since her feet had been bound at the age of three. But her mother-in-law claimed they were too big and badly shaped. When she pulled Hehua's toes straight by force then bent them further toward the arches, Hehua was not only forbidden to cry in pain, but had to smile and practice how to say "mother" in the most respectful, grateful, and affectionate tone. "You're lucky to have such a kind-hearted mother-in-law like me," she told Hehua. "When I came to the Wu family at your age, my mother-in-law broke every toe to reshape my feet, then ordered me to kneel in the yard to practice how to say mama from morning till night." So Hehua went through exactly the same routines as her mother-in-law did when she was a child daughter-in-law: getting up at dawn to grind corn and wheat, weaving, sowing, feeding pigs and chickens, cooking, and going to bed after midnight. At eleven, she was ordered to sleep in her husband's room. At eighteen, she had her first period and her first baby the next year.

After she had a son, she began talking back to her mother-in-law. Gradually, she hit back when her husband tried to beat her up. She was young and strong, and ready to risk her life in the fight, so she always won. Her husband sold his land to pay off his gambling debts and rarely came home. Hehua raised her children by weaving cloth and selling it at the fairs, and sowing wedding dresses and graveclothes for the villagers. One day her husband came home. Hehua locked the door and said mockingly, "What are you doing here? Nothing left to sell, except for the three mouths waiting to be fed. If you touch my kids, I'll kill you. Oh yes, you can sell me, if you have the guts."

She didn't realize that her husband, cornered by his debt, had already sold her to six men who were brothers and cousins. They lived in a mountain village and no one could afford a wife for himself. So they collected 150 silver yuan and bought a woman to bear children and carry on their family name. Hehua's husband warned them that his wife was known as a tigress, that they should be prepared for a good fight. The men waved their ropes and yokes, and said, "What wife? You've taken our money. Now she's ours. Even if she's a monster, we know how to handle her. Show us the way."

It was said that Hehua, mother of my great grandma, scratched four faces, broke three fingers, dug out two eyes, and bit off one nose before she was tied up and carried into the mountain like a captured wild sow. She was never seen or heard from again.

Hehua's mother, the grandma of my great-grandma, had a peculiar name, Shi Niang—"a picked up woman." A peasant found her one winter morning on the steps of the village temple, crying over a dead body. She didn't know where she came from, what she was called, who her real parents were. Her only memory was of traveling around many places with the dead man, whom she called father. But he wasn't really her father. They begged for food by singing songs. The peasant took her home and gave her to his son, who couldn't find a wife because of his baldness. Although she was given the name Shi Niang on her wedding day, everyone insisted on calling her "Baldhead's so-and-so." She had a few years of good life until her father-in-law, then her husband, died. She had no right to live in the house because she had no son. Her husband's relatives first sold her daughter to the Zhou family, who then sold her to a high-class brothel in Beijing. They made a good deal because Shi Niang was only twenty-one years old, stunningly beautiful, and an excellent singer. It was said that she became very successful. Even the emperor visited her in disguise.

The thread breaks at Shi Niang. All the techniques I have used to write this family tree—interviewing, investigating, story-telling, imagining, and creating—become useless. There are only five generations on paper. After much consideration, I decided to add my sisters and myself to the tree.

Wang Yan . . . the youngest sister . . . brought up by our aunts and Waipo till junior high . . . went to a banking college . . . excellent in math, swimming, and dancing . . . madly in love with her teacher . . . married with a son . . . secret relationship for six years . . . but the man ran off to Germany with her sister . . . heartbroken . . . couldn't understand how her own sister and her lover could do such a thing . . . finally married a fat man . . . became an expert in cooking, sewing, and house cleaning . . . firmly believes in the importance of a home, and wifely virtues . . . the key to keeping a marriage working . . .

Wang Haixia . . . the second sister . . . the most beautiful and promising child in the family . . . hated school . . . married once . . . divorced for giving birth to a girl . . . homeless . . . went to Beijing . . . Wang Yan asked her boyfriend to get her a job in his company . . . the man seduced her . . . took her to Germany with him . . . beat her up every day . . . Haixia called me from Germany for help . . . wanted to come to America . . . couldn't get a visa . . . took my advice to fight back . . . scratched the man's face several times . . . called the police for help . . . it worked . . . the man divorced his wife and married Haixia . . . still wondering why he degrades himself with a divorced woman . . . Haixia still waiting for her American visa . . . .

Wang Ping . . . first daughter . . . already a sin . . . plus ugly and stubborn . . . no one's favorite . . . grew up with Waipo . . . worked three years in the countryside in order to go to college . . . studied and taught English at a foreign language school . . . finally dream came true . . . went to Beijing University . . . first love . . . a married man with two children . . . five years of secrecy . . . problems with authority . . . problems with men . . . can't obey . . . can't say no . . . torn inside . . . start lying in order to survive . . . married to get out of the first relationship . . . marriage lasted a week . . . broke up in the middle of the honeymoon . . . returned to Beijing homeless . . . thought of coming to New York as a way out . . . received an MA from Long Island University . . . . found a job at board of education . . . started writing poetry and stories . . . granted a green card . . . still searching for something else . . . .

I guess I must be an ungrateful beast.
Compared to everyone else, I'm the luckiest woman in the family.
To quote my boyfriend,
"You have sexy legs,
pretty breasts,
a lovely face,

and a good brain.
So what the hell are you still angry about?"

Yes, I guess I should feel lucky.

My sister in China still plays the role of an obedient wife and
    filial daughter-in-law,
whereas I can make fun of the old Chinese Women's Comm-
    andments and create my own rule book about men.
It goes like this:

1. Men always seek an ideal woman: she is a mother and child at once, soft and strong at the same time; she must be a virtuous model to other men, but act like a whore in his bed.

2. Men often complain that women tie them down to the earth. But when they are left alone, instead of achieving transcendence, they wear themselves out in drunkenness and competition.

3. Men are never ever to be trusted with your heart, and if unfortunately you fall in love with one, don't tell him.

4. If a man asks you for money, don't ever give it to him.

5. If you ask a man for money and he acts cheap, sell his richest possession and leave at once.

6. Your greatest strength is that every man believes that he is indispensable and knows every woman's need.

I can laugh as much as I want,

but I still feel like screaming inside.

I still depend upon the skills I was taught since my birth,

the skills to lie to men,

to scheme and be wily

as well as to please and charm.

I still have a master,

whose caprices control my sentiments and acts.

I must scream, even though I have no voice.

Since my birth, silence has been my single weapon.

Now it no longer suffices.

The need to speak

leaves me restless like a hunger.

My words may not say what I mean,

but they're my only means.

I must scream through my voiceless throat,

even if I have to burp and fart,

and suffer from chronic diarrhea.

I don't care.

I'm tearing myself and this world apart,

to find out why I'm still angry.

Splintered Eye

As I kneel bleeding away
I hear your cry from underground.
I stare at your blue eyelids
and the words on your cheeks:
There's a sleeping wolf in everyone's head.
Soul is a gigantic stomach, you once said,
in which the burning desire combats hopelessly
the calculation of reason.
The ambiguity of human life
lies between mad laughter and sobbing tears.
No one can explain
why the child gathers stones
to build castles only to destroy.

To console my pain,
you told me the dream of a stone
which abandoned itself to the anguish of death.
You laughed at those
who don't know darkness even though
they wallow in it.
Pain is nothing
but a mediator between love and hate,
a measurement for civilization.
We are closer to a mushroom,
a packet of baking yeast and mold on cheese
than to God.

In order to chase the sun
a bee drives itself crazy.
The lover runs here and there.
She weeps and howls.
She beats herself on the chest.
She takes new measures and plots against herself.
She doesn't want to know
that the only way for survival
is to wait,
to wait and betray,
to forget.
In order to love,
she is dying of excess
of the tension of memory.
Love is heavy, heavier than death.
And heaviness destroys love.

She sits on the brownstone steps, staring at the twilight without blinking. Her short curly hair clings to her scalp like a cat sinking her teeth into the bone of a prey. She sits there, like a sinister messenger of the night, on the steps of a brownstone.

I walk toward her against my will. She draws me, sucking me into her blank eyes. I reach out my hand. I touch her knee with my fingertip. She continues staring at the sunset, her eyes, the only color, change from hazel to orange. A stream trickles down the steps, warm, clear steam rising from the flowing water like the morning mist. I trace it to its origin.

Our eyes meet for the first time. She is laughing, her eyes now the color of the piss. "I want you to abandon yourself like this," she orders in her silence. The piss makes a pool around my feet.

Daddy,
I'm coming home naked,
with footprints all over my body.
No need to cry for me—
I'm still the ruler of hearts.

Last night I dreamed of taking off my clothes on the street and lying down between two men on a mattress. They scolded me for being shameless. I laughed and said: "It's because you have a dirty mind."

So resurrection isn't just a myth.
You lived as though you were dying
in order to achieve eternity.
To refuse to be devoured by fear,
you flung yourself onto the track.
Not that dying is hateful,
but living servilely is a sin.
Only I know
your heart is higher than the sky,
with a fate thinner than paper.
The greatest agony is not always betrayed by cries.
Nothing can cover the passion
beneath your blue eyelids,
the passion that has no spectator.

No need to be ashamed.
You're my brother
and I love your smile
even though it's splintered into
ten thousand pieces.

drowned . . . in the waves of nausea . . . entering infinity . . . to
embrace the sun . . . ready to burn into ashes . . . no heart . . . no soul
. . . only the tender tongue . . . to die in order to love . . . to rip one-
self from oneself . . . soul swallowed by lust . . . lifted in such a way
. . . . to the light . . . never in the light . . . hands reaching out . . .
who heard the pitiful cry . . . torn from the ground . . . love is but a
subjunctive mood . . . it's over . . . never over . . . love without con-
dition . . . .

Once I had a fight with mother.
I told her: "I'll never talk to you again."
With a smile she replied: "I bet you'll come back in two hours."
I walked away and hid in my room.
I read. I listened to music. I called up every person in my address book.
It was still only an hour and forty-three minutes.
I opened mother's door and stood at the threshold.
"Silly girl," she said, "don't fight with your mom any more. It's useless."
I asked: "How did you know I'd return?"
"Because I created you with my soul."

So you threw yourself in,
without principal, without reservation,
just as you flung your body

onto the track.

You have no regret. You've loved.

nothing to regret . . . have tried the best . . . always the best
. . . rushed toward that place . . . ignored so many tender
calls . . . that beautiful place . . . took away all the space . . .
in the soul . . . but one day . . . someone spoke . . . it was all
an illusion . . . this self-exile . . . how long can one stand . . .
in order to live . . . mother said . . . the heart must be colder
than steel . . . tried the best . . . no more regret . . . no more
cry for fate . . . no more self-pity . . . heaven or hell . . . no
between . . . no compromise . . . .

Real pain is unspeakable.

If it can be described or talked about,

it's no longer real.

Mother told her daughter: "Happy people are weak. They are
like clouds without a base or weight. I forbid you to be happy.
Make your heart as cold as iron, in order to live."

In the rebuilt wooden house,

I forget the wood,

forget the only window in front of me.

I stand in the manner of a tree,

my feet covered with fruit

but I can't pick one up.

So this is life—

forever on the point of no return

forever in a process

of losing our treasures.

When I was a kid, my parents always fought at dusk. I hid behind the door and watched the sunset through my tear-soaked hands. I made myself a pledge: "My children will never go through this, never."

The pork in my stomach started moaning, bleeding, and growing. It soon filled each organ in my body and turned me into a piece of raw meat. I woke up with diarrhea.

Mother
Tell me how to draw a line
between multiplicity and schizophrenia.
Tell me how to tell directions
at night.
Tell me if it's true
that the eye sees more
than the heart.

I lean on your shoulder
my callused hands in your white hair
that came with your birth.
The tide is rising
to flood your eyes.

And finally everything will
turn into a still life—
the cities, the forests,
the noble and the humble, you and me—
all quiet like ashes—caught in the light.

The past will rise to the level of the present.

Beginning and end will merge as one.

But not now, not yet,

not till your cry

has wiped out all the efforts

of carefully controlled words.

Punctual Arrival

When a new life cries
And the neighbor comes over with a lantern,
My heart feels heavy
As if witnessing a wedding
Unable to consider its own ending.

Before we lie down
In the earth,
We cannot avoid any misgiving.

Winter is blowing its horn.
You set off, bare-handed.
The fields extend—
A scroll of calligraphy.
No matter how our eyes see things,
Their importance does not depend
      on our existence.

No reason
To blame the weather for my arthritis.
I refuse to let my mother
Read my palms.

Wind has torn
The last button off my shirt.

Desire burns
Through the exposed skin.

I still love to look up at the sky
Even though there's no bird flying.

In front of the crying baby,
I can only say:
"Send me a postcard from your journey."

Transference

Did you dream last night?
You asked, a routine question of the morning.

Yes, I meant to say, but kept silent,
brushing my hair over your bowl of cereal.

Did you hear me sobbing
like a baby before she learns to smile?

Did you hear me shouting:
I want to change my name to LeRoy?

My professor gave me a ride behind his bike
and had a fit after he arrived.

My last dream crawled into your broken tooth,
it hurt so much you had to take the day off.

Dreams endless, no way to express.
To speak or not speak, no longer a question.

You sipped your coffee and turned to the window.

Outside there was overnight laundry on the clothesline

and sparrows among grape vines.

Your patience stuck, like birds in the rain.

A river is made under the ground.

Shall I fold a bird to fly over my head?

It's no miracle

  to catch up with my parents at such an early age.

I close my book

  like closing an angel's gaze.

Now, thirty-seven years old,

  allergic to almost everything,

I shift my obsession to writing letters

where things have a time, place, name

  but no need to explain.

Need for Uncertainty

Against the screen of the western wall
a moth flutters its striped wings.
Anonymous grass grows fat in the rain.
It nudges travelers
into discount malls.
Children, sighing, pick up books from under beds.
You bring in wood to light a fire.
I listen to your murmuring speech
through the bathroom keyhole,
but can't make out a word.

Summer crawls away with care,
splashing out endless baby's breath on the skylight.
Smoke escapes through the chimney—
its smell expands the damp air.
Someone is smashing dishes again.
Everything under control—
we didn't fight this Sunday,
and made love to *Thirty-six Fillet.*

Fated to be together
like canned sardines—
bones against bones,
but never meet.

In this glass cell,
things can be seen from different directions.

I take a deep breath and hold it
in my pubic region.
The grass outside the walls
is making its last chlorophyll of the day.

Crossing Essex

River under clouds
Mountains in the distance

Crossing Essex
arm in arm
two teenage girls
lips half open
deep in their pink dreams
A white-haired baby
stumbles toward his hapless mother
An old man freezes in the middle of traffic
No one listens to the sun
No one follows the river
The light turns red

River of yellow cabs

The first woman and man
jumped off Nuwa's hand
Repaired heavens
Ten thousand years of sleep
Sitting by the river
she smiled at her last mission

They waded into the water
Shadows sank to the bottom

Earth burnt off the last rays
Their bodies turned into maps

The river is no obstacle

The young Jews walk whispering past Wong's Kodak Express
their beards float
their pants slip below their belly buttons
Through his window of cosmetics
the old man winks at the teenagers
Women chatter at Guss Pickles
The sweet and sour smell drifts
toward Williamsburg Bridge
Underneath a man stares at his broken bottle of coconut milk
oozing into the subway grill
A bee buzzes around the huge bare waist of the homeless
I suddenly understand why Ted Berrigan took speed

Summer Rain

An incomplete moon broke through branches
kneading me into shadows on the window
The sun died in my dream last night
Fog rose from moldy benches
I touched your shoulder, said I'm sorry
Even cats are afraid of loneliness

Forty-one days of rain
You mumbled it was time
to make a boat
When I turned my head
you started dancing "Fernando's" tango
waving a red scarf on the balcony
I passed a man peeing between buildings
frightened by the echoes of my own footsteps

When the rain stopped
Tompkin Square Park residents climbed out
to mend their plastic tents with clothes pins
and sweep their ratty carpets within fences
I walked toward the Manhattan Bridge
to see the Chinese bag lady
behind her lace curtain

Haiku Trio

FIRST LOVE

To show her he was a man,
he underwent the fire department exam
and died of a heart attack in the process.

BLESSING

My mother, sitting on a turtle
with a snake around her neck, announced my fortune:
The star of your husband won't shine till you're fifty.

A FLASH OF THOUGHT FROM THE RIVER

I really think I have nothing to do with humans
though I occasionally drown a few
to remind them of their origin.

Mirror Images

I

Standing alone in the fields,
Alone—I do not feel cold.

An old tree, having missed the season of blossoms,
Enters dusk at the horizon.

The cooking smoke has faded above the peasants' huts,
Revealing the golden haystacks in the back.

An old peasant in the yard
Ties his wheat stalks into bundles of firewood.

Chicks linger in the weeds, forgetting to return
When the sun shadow reaches the top of the clay wall.

Now the old man sits facing the ocean,
Watching dusk curdle his garden into a still life.

A plough cuts into soil far away,
And folds a black pattern onto the empty land.

At night I emerge from my body dancing at will,
And tell the panicked world I'm just sleepwalking.

II

Stars are visionary notes,
eyes drawn upward.

Poplars applaud each breeze.
Songs make a home at the end of my sight.

Wild geese return from the north—how their wings stir the air!
I pull a feather to measure their routes.

Cat Buckwheat crawls among clovers, his white tail
knocking dew drops down the symmetrical three-leaves.

Among the heated battle between two invisible cats,
pear blossoms pour into the blue sky.

Action leaks everywhere, like an exposed wire.
Words short into silence.

This Land

rugged, unforgiving,

life imprinted on rocks,

the living images

of trees, plants, and shark's teeth,

petrified, then tumbling down into soil.

Mountains churned by ancient seas,

where eagles dwell, fearless, humans cannot reach.

On the side of the cliff

ancient Anazasis built homes.

Sky of forever,

rocks stick out tongues for speech,

but there is absolute silence in Frijoles Canyon.

Unnamed

for Adam

When you drive three hundred miles a day,
and camp out eight nights straight,
the body begins to do its own cleaning.
In Sante Fe, people dwell in red clay houses
under the sky forever blue.
The Taos Pueblos live under the constant gaze of tourists
for a life that has no tap water or electricity.
A dollar a person to peek inside their bedrooms—a living museum.
I passed by the Indian Institute of Arts,
no trace or smell of my beloved.
You say you don't know Wittgenstein or Heidegger,
and you dislike naming.
But no matter.
Things have no need to be called under the clouds,
they all find a place with or without names.
In the end, books, cities,
our passions and great tragedies—
all petrified into rocks.
What is five thousand years of human history
compared to the age of the earth?
We think we're in control,
but the power lies elsewhere.

No Sense of Direction

So just like this . out of the plane at Kennedy . Destination Flushing address . no sense of direction . what? . a quarter for the pay phone . no . all her luggage . Twenty-five dollars and a dictionary . first night in basement . sleepless . indigestion of dreams . want to scream but . no . her sponsor upstairs . silent night . staring into space . no sense of direction . hover between awareness and loss . first month working to pay off the plane ticket . selling Chinese antiques . Fifth Avenue . leaves falling on the homeless blanket . on the golden canopy of the store . "Two Worlds" . Pizza for lunch . on the boss . first bite of cheese . throwing up on the boss' shoes . no sense of value . no brain for business . too stubborn to be a running dog . out of the store . out of the basement . out hunting for jobs . two restaurants . Flushing for weekend . midtown from Monday to Friday . first apartment room in Bay Ridge . $180 for rent . four hours underground . reading *Ulysses* in train . or dozing . rocking like a cradle . mother rocker . sleeping in class . sorry Shakespeare . tender mercies . full time school or get out of America . lost in Time Square . "Someone give me a quarter please" . no sense of direction . Malaysian Chinese landlady . dream of becoming a fashion designer . furious at the question if she was lonely . kicked out the next week . $250 a room at Elmhurst from a Taiwanese couple . can't afford it . divorced engineer offers to pay half . offers to take her to the Jersey mall . her nose pressed against the window . looking into the consuming world . "Buy whatever you want" . as if dreams come true . what's the price . enter her room at night and carry her into his bed . more offers . a home . a car . a marriage . a green card . he snoring . bad breath . stare into space . sleepless . indigestion of the soul . no sense of direction . sit staring at her hands . infected with athlete's foot . suddenly see them wet . teardrops . what? . no! . no time for pity . too proud to sell . move to Harlem . where she belongs . different root . same fate. $100 . through a Chinese girlfriend . married for green card . thought she could settle down for a while . but in the third week someone turned the key in the lock at midnight . the owner . no . the lover of the Chinese girl . back from an interview in San Francisco . sold for a hundred . no more girlfriend . not available . another offer . one night shelter and a screw . "stinky meat" she was told after the business . in the dark . long after . tongue in the cheek . no speech possible . suddenly she realizes . gradually I realize . so much need for love . no time for love . this awful thought . drifting in and out . make it stop . God is love . What? . no! . no God for Chinese . sick of belief . but this need for love . no money for love . that December afternoon . roaming along Fifth Avenue . a job . waitress . bus girl . cashier . a place to stay . a bowl of instant noodles . grabbing at the straw . nothing there . on to the next . in the December snow . no sense of direction . feelings dismissed . how she survived . but this roar . this voice in her skull . this need to be loved . falling on her face . in the first snow . tender mercies . in the December snow . in the unheated basement . Jackson Heights . first night . flooded bathroom . floating mattress . yeast infection . punishment for the sin . face in her hands . avoiding a curious rat . on the eve of the Chinese New . what? . no? . OK . on the eve of Christ . no? . what? . New Year? . Good God! . sorry . good heaven . no God for Chinese . New Year's Eve . a rat sitting on my face . waiting . silence . Big Apple rising . trumpets blowing . something wet in hands . hers probably . no one else around . except for the rat . dear rat . Happy New Year . phone ringing . her sponsor's call . "ungrateful beast" . telling the story of the Harlem apartment to a journalist . how can Chinese betray Chinese . shame . no more connection . she is on her own . she has been on her own . only pretending she has someone behind her . Big Apple rising . no more

dreams . no head . no brain . no sense of direction . only se-
quences of the apartments . six . what? . ten . Good God . sorry
. good heaven . memories fading . last stop Flushing address .
life recycles . time compressed . fragments of names . being
achieved silence . images incapable of repose . asserting like
maddened . recognizable even burned into ashes . clinging to
the threshold . one has to believe something . face in her
hands . tender mercies . on New Year's Eve . no sense of direc-
tion . no direction .

Song of Calling Souls

THE DROWNED VOICES FROM THE *GOLDEN VENTURE*

So here we are
    in the evening darkness
    of Rose Hill Cemetery
gazing out from our ghosts
    like the homeless outside windows.
No moon,
    the spring not the spring of the old days.
Our bodies not ours,
    but only bodies rotting
    in the grave of lao fan.
We look at the sky
    the earth
    and the four directions.
The storm gathers in
    from all sides.
How shall we pass through this night?

The wind comes blowing.
    We six
in deep shadow
    stand at the end of time,
stand in the night
    that is not just an absence of light,
but a persistent voice,
    unsteady and formless,
hum of summer crickets.

Something wants to be said,
    even if our words
grasp the air in vain
    and nothing remains.

Our story has set a fact
    beyond fable
Our story
    has no beginning or end.

"Home," we say,
and before we utter the word,
our voices choke with longing:

    The cliff of Fuzhou
        studded with stiff pines.
    The waters of Changle
        shadowed in the sway of bamboo.
    Sea and sky fused.
        Mystic fires along the shore.
    Fishermen's dwellings everywhere.

        How lovely!
        How familiar!

When dusk falls,
    faint seagull cries.
Blue smoke rises
    from red-tiled roofs.
Small boats offshore
    and fishhawks in silhouette.
Salty winds
    carrying the murmur of reeds.
Tide roads of the sea.

The scenes grow in memory,
scenes we lived day by day,
paying no mind:

Generation after generation,
    nets cast into the lingering light,
    seeds planted in the morning mist.
Fishing kept us out on the waves.
Farming bound our women to the soil.

But at times
    we heard a voice, a promise,
        a golden dream.
Things seen and heard
    turned to confusion.
We pulled our boats onto shore,
    left our wives and children
    behind the mountain's shadow.

From village to village
    we bought and sold
anything at hand
    socks underwear suits dresses gold even drugs
seven days a week
    three hundred sixty-five days a year
and not just for the money:
    the yearning for adventure
    ran deep in our veins.
We played hide-and-seek
    with the government and police.
When we got caught and lost all our earnings
    we called ourselves "Norman Bethune."
If Mao were still alive
    he'd have surely praised us
    as he did that Canadian doctor
    who gave his life
    helping us fight the Japanese ghosts.

We were glad
	to help build a "socialist" China
	with our illegal gains.
Anyway we had a good laugh
	over our losses.
Still, waves of desire
	rose daily,
this voice luring
	from the far side of the sea.
Not that we yearned for gold
	or worldly delights,
but this voice
	first muttering
	then roaring in our heads.

So in hope and fear we fared.
	In tears we fared.
Mist spread a veil
	till ocean-bound.
Pinewood mirrored
	in deep green.
At the bottom of the *Golden Venture*
	we did not see our women weeping
	did not hear our children calling.
Only the voice
	"Kari, kari . . . "
of wild geese.

We sailed the ocean
	in the hold of the *Golden Venture*
		pigs chickens dogs snakes,
	whatever it was they called us.
Our bodies not ours,
	sold to the "snakeheads" for the trip.

You ask why we did this?
    Ask the geese why they migrate
        from north to south,
    why the eels swim thousands of miles
        to spawn in the sea.
Tides of desire
    rise for no reason.
so we fared with the faith
    New York had more *fu* than Fuzhou,
    people there enjoyed "perpetual happiness"
    like the name of *Changle.*
So we sailed with the belief
    we could buy ourselves back for $30,000
        within three years.
    Our hard work would bring freedom
        to the next generation.
    Our sons would be prosperous and happy,
        not like us, cursed
        by our own country, cursed
        by the "old barbarians."
    America needed our labor and skills
        as much as we needed its dream . . .

And here we are,
    hovering around this New Jersey cemetery.
Or bodies gone,
    but our blind souls still hanging
        like curtains soaked in rain.

        Our summer clothes so thin!
        So thin our dreams!

Hovering,
    that dark night near Rockaway,
our ship finally heaving into sight of New York.

In thirst and hunger we waited.
In fear and hope we waited
    to be lifted from the ship's hold
    and alight on the land of paradise.

"Jump," we'd been told,
"once your feet touch American soil
    you'll be free." In the dark rain we waited.
"Jump," someone shouted,
"the ship is sinking, the police are coming!"
so we jumped
    into the night
    into the raging sea,
our breasts smothered
    by foam and weeds,
our passions tangled,
    the breath beaten from our bodies
by despair and hate.

        Oh, we've sunk so low!
        We've sunk so low!

Only to rise again,
    for clinging to wrongful things.
Easy to sink
    in the fire of desire.
Regret comes after the deed.
    Sorrow!
Our former days now changed,
    leaving no trace.
The distant mountain lies alone.
Shadows of the city so far away.
    Sorrow!
We can speak only in weeping,
memory nothing but white hair on the heart.

Condemned to wander,
lost among the roots of our six senses,
gazing at New York,
gazing homeward.
Fuzhou's mighty waves roiling through the night,
bride in green unveiled in scarlet chamber,
lovers' pillows joined like Siamese twins.

Who can avoid sorrow in this world?

Our legs lingering
    in the dew-drenched grass
here and there, still clinging.
This deep night,
    is it outside-this-world?
Our women and children
    still awaiting our return.
But here we are,
    nameless,
in life and after life,
    apart.
Our song is the crane
    calling in her cage
when she thinks of her young
    toward nightfall.
Will it reach Fuzhou and Changle
    and stir souls from their sleep?
On the boat
    we were close,
hundreds of us in the hold
    jammed in and in.
Here we live even closer,
    six bodies in one hole,

the earth sifting into
 our common grave,
unmarked,
 no stone erected
then crumbling.
 Sands of the shore
may reach an end,
 but not our grief.

Home, oh go home!
 An empty wave.
Ten thousand voices,
 broadcast the pain.
Please, oh please
 call our names
    Chen Xinhan, Zhen Shimin
even if you can't say them right
    Lin Guoshui, Chen Dajie
even if you don't know
 our origin or age
    Wang Xin, Huang Changpin
Please, oh please
 call us.
Raise our shadows
 from the moss.
Be gentle
 as you call our names.
Do not wake us by force.
 But call us.
Do not let us fade
 from this place,
unlit and unfulfilled.

Endless Embrace

This year
the garden trees
    bore only one peach
young grapes dried
    along vines
and starlings made love till late November
  amid morning glories

And on Thanksgiving
    back and forth on the ferry
    joints swollen with unspoken words
The sun goes down
    a basketball of mandarins

So many stories
    no place to begin
Memory, at last, becomes a path

    And you came along
Hands on breasts
your leopard-like skin, heap of mane
    And I made you promise
not to abandon me
to the gang of enemies within

I've fallen into strange habits
and I've done terrible things
    stalking the earth
    treacherous, full of jealousy
    always ready to sting

    And by sheer accident
I stepped on your footprint
    and turned into a nymph

74

To lean on you
    I felt no shame
    Alone
I can take the curse from hell
    but not this heavenly weight
Oh, to accept me,
    it was right
    to accept me and then never leave

Waves, quiver of trees
glitter of mirrors, flicker
of ears, vision after vision
of imaginary wars, characters
written on air, and gates to blessing
Add more blue to blues
    or strike me with a sunbolt
This time she's not begging,
this China woman, pigheaded,
        no longer a mistress

We'd like to think
    a mongoloid knows no envy or jealousy
After an intense feeding on dips and chips
Benny sang for Thanksgiving:
    Mom Boon Haap (whistle)
    Birr Mieu Daaa (fingers across mouth)
    Cad Bog Woon (clap hands)

Zhong gua de gua
Zhong dou de dou
"Plant melons and you get melons
Sow beans and you get beans"
But even Chinese sayings
    however ancient
    wear away

It was Thanksgiving
    van lost in Jersey City
A fat moon hung low
    over Manhattan's silhouette
Hallucination of my father, out there,
    calling my name—
        Fifty years in Shanghai
        still kept his Shandong accent

And love, lost in the prospect of losing
Roses fading, overnight,
    in the bottle of Fischer D'Alsace
People say I'm definitely a masochist
But aches and grief
    keep me alert
And I don't fear bleeding
    from time to time

I tried to grow a garden
    but neglected to tend the soil
Now I must learn
    the art of feeling
  nearest things
                unfamiliar

To walk around
    thinking no evil
To live—with gratitude abundant
    and no less passion

To speak, not out of sorrow,
    but in wonder

Ultimate Passage

You need a good heart and strong lungs
to enter Tibet, my guide said.
Do you have them?

I'm just looking for a bridge
to cross from the seen to the unseen.

Someone stole my bag the day before I flew to China, stripping me of all my American I.D.s and bank cards.

The ship arrived at the island of Dinghai at 3:15 A.M. No one was available to pilot us to the port. We waited for dawn in the middle of the East China sea.

Having been away for twenty years, I returned home on a *sanlun,* a three-wheeled bike with a carriage in the back for passengers.

Here and there I recognized a few buildings. Everything had changed yet remained the same.

Outside my mother's apartment, two women were selling frogs, flayed, bleeding, yet still wriggling on skewers. When I raised my camera, they shook their frogs to demonstrate how alive their merchandise was.

Here on the island, I ate three bowls of rice each meal and never worried about getting fat. My stomach grew but no one cared.

On the street, a gray-haired woman mimicked twenty passersby within a minute. She was similar, not similar to something or somebody. She was just similar.

Even though I have a Chinese passport, I still have to pay the double, even triple for hotels and plane tickets as a foreigner would. I have become a "foreign devil" by living in New York for ten years.

People get up at five or six to do xiang gong exercises in parks. It produces the smell of musk and flowers from mysterious sources. *Xiang!* people shout when they catch a whiff.

When my aunt-in-law in Shanghai handed me the book of *Xiang Gong,* my nostrils were filled with the aroma of musk. Everyone in the room said that I'd been drawn to this art by fate.

I arrived in the rainy season. Mold grew on my face amid the constant drizzle. I lay in the bed where my father died, afraid to fall into dreams where two Korean women kept chasing me with knives.

I thought I'd given all I could, even more than I could.

I speak my thoughts aloud to my beloved
without hearing myself.

Every working member in my grandma's family is involved in business. They can't understand why, at my age, I'm still going to school and writing poetry.

Poet Mo Fei is a gardener in Beijing. He doesn't know how to make money or find things in his house. But he knows every book that comes into the bookstores. My mother took a look at him and suggested that if he ever wanted to be rich, he first had to remove the mole on the side of his nose.

Born into the dream time between,
what then shall we take for the real?
The waves of capitalism
cut through our time like shears.
Doubt is for mortals.
And yet who has not fallen into desire?

Tell me your story, your real story.
This is the only way I can know you.
We are each a biography.
I keep small things in my heart
even though they seem to be weightless.

The ship sounded its foghorns into Shanghai Port, lined with western industrial plants and equipment. History is fond of circles. A crowd of young men whistled catcalls as their ship glided past. I didn't know which way to turn my head. I sat on the top deck the whole night watching the moon rise and set in the sea. My brother Hu drank beer with a Wenzhou businessman who owned a wholesale engine store in Shanghai. Hu had been trying to open a business himself, but never succeeded. It's your fault, he teased me. You never stopped reading as a child, and we all followed your steps. Now my brain is damaged by books. I said nothing, just laughing and picking at the food the businessman had bought for us: boiled shrimp, pickled mud snails, steamed butterfish, goose and seashells. I had disguised myself as a country woman, but the businessman still recognized me as an overseas Chinese.

I can fake my words, but not my expressions.

I told my grandma my first book was dedicated to her, but she had nothing to say. Her heart was broken when she learned I needed two more years to finish my dissertation. She kept muttering: too bad my granddaughter is so honest, too bad she's a bookworm, until I muttered back: too bad my grandma loves money more than me. It shut her up. I rewarded her with a 1,000-yuan banquet.

At Chengdu, I bought a bottle of sunblock for 372 yuan, 72 yuan more than my brother's monthly salary.

She announced, as she shelled out eight hundred dollars for a coat: money is a woman's guts after she reaches forty.

She lost her prescription sunglasses, but I didn't offer to look for them.

Rain and wind on the Great Wall,
and intense selling under the wall.
I overheard two soaked tourists say:
You're not a man unless you've climbed the Great Wall,
but when you get there, you're just a fool.

I've had it with tourist scenes, he shouted from beneath his umbrella in his one-yuan disposable plastic rain coat.

Going to bathroom in China was such an adventure.
He kept dreaming about it after he returned to New York.

The lights went out and the elevator stopped between the floors of a Beijing apartment building on a hot summer night. "Oh, the operator is getting back at us again for taking the elevator without her," a passenger observed in the pitch dark. He screamed nonstop, almost yanking my arm out of its joint. When we finally got out, he crouched on a sofa, drenched in sweat, unable to speak for hours. My sister couldn't stop laughing. "It happens at least once a week, just like our homemade dish. How can you be working in Beijing if you're scared of this? I thought Americans were great heroes." He shouted back: Don't you know anything about phobia? But my sister didn't know the word even though she spoke some English.

I went back to Beijing University to see the dormitory washing room.

The same smell and basins of laundry under taps,

as if the ten-year gap had never existed,

as if I were again dragged out of the hallway in my dreams.

The only real thing was the sign at the gate:

No male visitors allowed!

I peeked into my old window on my toes,

and was frightened by the appearance of a girl with painted eyebrows.

Welcome, she smiled, and talked to me in English

despite my Chinese face.

The silent, nocturnal part of me

communicates only through dreams.

The invisible often casts more light on things.

I grow old fast on this land.

He Zhong, a poet and editor of *Tibetan Tour*, the son of the Yugu tribal chieftain, a pure bastard so he claimed, being of mixed Tibetan, Mongolian, Turkish, and Chinese, patted his chest to guarantee our entrance to Tibet.

I borrowed my sister's I.D. to disguise myself as a Chinese.
We don't look alike, but no matter. Only the paper matters.

Identity is a fiction.
I exist as a rush of perceptions.
My memory becomes a heap of garbage
and sickness part of me.
For all these years I could speak only through pain,
searching for some ultimate harmony.
Yet only through pain and sorrow did life come to me.

How much does one have to suffer
to become beautiful?
And even beauty does not please all the time.

I want a car, she declared at the dinner, so I can drive to New
Jersey to buy untaxed seltzer.

He gave up his position
as a leading violinist in China's major orchestra
and came to New York to play in the subways.
Who is to judge the worth of these things?
We've all gone astray in the flurry.
Who can judge the illusion?
Sometimes hope alone is enough
after the remains of a great love.
The driving passion, the terrible fear of loss,
now a fleeting sound from strings.

I dreamed of becoming a Buddha by throwing myself into a river. My mentor was surprised with my success because the odds are one out of a million. A jeep hurtled toward a girl. I changed its course with my newly-gained power. The girl was saved. I died from exhaustion. Immediately I began another incarnation. When I was awakened, I was turning into a serpent with a Buddha's head.

The hottest summer food at Sichuan and northern China is fondue. You sit around a table with a gas stove in the middle, surrounded by dishes of raw duck tongues, gizzards, pig brains, duck blood, potatoes, sprouts, wood ear vegetables, eels, loach, watermelon seeds, tofu, instant noodles, lotus, beef stripes, ham, mushroom and beltfish. You dip the morsels in the sizzling soup and then pop them into your mouth.

No one spoke English at this business banquet. He got their attention by asking for a glass of scotch whiskey. The restaurant didn't have any. Totally embarrassed, the host ordered a bottle of gujing gong, one of the best Chinese spirits. After two cups, he pretended to be drunk and made a funny scene, howling along with a popular karaoke love song called "Xiao Fang," which he didn't know a word of, except for *xie xie*—thank you.

At the farewell dinner before my flight to Lhasa, the head of the Tibet Commodity Bureau, a yogi, looked at me, closed his eyes, and saw a Tara rising from my body. He predicted that I'd find religion in my forties.

I experienced my first altitude sickness in the bathroom of Lhasa Airport, face to face with a woman squatting over the toilet, her door wide open, her private parts all exposed.

No trees or grass on the mountains here, not even soil.

So close to the sky, so far from the earth: Tibet.

In Beijing, Doctor Zhang fixed up his back with a wooden chisel, but he threw it out again dancing to Madonna in a Lhasa karaoke cafe.

On the sidewalk I saw an old peasant woman clinging to a tree.
Steadily she breathed in the dust kicked up by the trucks, cars, and tractors.
She clung to the tree, crooked, still green, her head covered with a faded white towel.
Suddenly the island dialect, all the stories that were lost in me, returned.

Western science calls the elimination of right and wrong "equalization"—the ultimate sickness, the ultimate destroyer of all words and selves. Buddhism calls this "enlightenment." The only difference lies in compassion.

"*Bu er*—same difference," replied the monk businessman when I asked him to explain how he could search for the spiritual and material worlds at the same time.

No one has called for months.
When the mind is full,
the room ceases to be empty.

Everything around me moves.

I look into this moment of stillness,
my vision splits like a fish.

When you dance, Mother said,
think of the blue sky, the positive air
that rushes into your body from eight directions.
Let the world seep in through your nose and pores.

Look, she said, a Buddha is forming in my palm.

I entered Tibet with a stiff neck.
But that's not the point. The point is
I have entered Tibet.

In Touch with America

There was a time
when I was full of plans
about what to do in America. Wear skirts and dresses all year round.
Meet a real gentleman who always opens doors and pulls chairs for me.
Marry a millionaire and have a bunch of kids.
Wear makeup, even mascara, and no one will call me *yaojin*—slut.
Make some women friends. Surely they'll like me better over there.
Drive across the country in a Cadillac.
Buy a loft in Manhattan, a beach house in the Outer Banks, and a farmhouse
under one of Colorado's snowcaps.
Say no to anyone whenever I want
and no one will ask me to dig into the bottom of my soul.
Every day will be a feast.
And my mother will never find out about any of this.

It took me ten years to figure out
that I'm totally allergic to cosmetics, and my eyelashes are too short for mascara.
Doctors advise me to wear thick pants to keep my legs warm from arthritis attack.
I met a guy who jumped up from the dinner table to attend me
whenever I made a slight movement.
He almost drove me insane.
So I walked out on him one day after I yelled: Let me piss in peace.
And I discover that rich men like to bathe themselves in heavy perfume
which gives me the worst headaches.

Ten years, and I still haven't learned how to drive.
Once I can say whatever I want, I realize I prefer silence.

Every day I run to my mailbox to see if my mother has written to me.
When a letter arrives, I leave it unopened for weeks on my desk.

I should tell you better now
how much is illusion.
But I still rather believe
fantasy is stronger than reality.
God punishes by giving us what we want.
And great beginnings don't always end well.
How can things grow
if you pull their roots?

Endless ache for life, however brief,
souls waiting to unfold.
The face of the sky, rich in joy and virtue,
hard to describe, yet we may still try to imitate,
like children.
I'm crazy about the ocean, and I love flying,
still I don't like my feet off the ground too long.
Love or hate with moderation,
if you don't want to be burnt to ashes.
But the navel of the earth
roars with an eternal fire.

No matter how high we jump,
we all have to obey the laws of the Mighty,

as the Flamenco master stamps her feet,
planting them firmly in the ground,
her body works with gravity, never against it.
When are we going to learn to live with nature
and detest any untimely growth?
In America people give Thanksgiving
to the land they love and fear.
But even if they have rescued all the Chinese babies
chained to cribs in the orphanage,
will things go back to normal?

Just like this
we torment ourselves
in the city.
The only feelings worth having
are ecstasy and despair.
Things so confused with a babble of tongues,
fear penetrates soul, screeching like bats.
I sleep but it is the night that dreams.
Only a mile of oxygen is left for our breathing,
but the city, ploughed with desire and sorrow,
grumbles and shouts for more.
Fire and smoke shoot up
through the subway grates
on the sidewalk of 42nd Street.
Love so scarce,
it becomes a miracle.

Are the gods also lonely?
Do they get their satisfaction
by looking over the death and temporality of their imitators?
After all, it's the pain and torment that keep us humane.
If this seems good to them,
we shall, in the course of suffering,
be made to avow our errors.

So let's sing about this unforgiveness.
Sing about hell, or this whole world,
all the stones, soil, wind, rain, clouds,
scorched cliffs and the lonely sun,
built to endure, but always in place,
which is good.
The smell of cedars and mushrooms along the stream,
the grizzly that killed a mother and her son in his rage,
the lightning that hit the photographer on top of Pike's Peak,
the sound of pine bark cracking and grasshoppers' wings,
mountains with folds like the wrinkles of an old saint's face,
and our mothers and fathers cutting wheat in the fields,
their backs smoking in the sun,
all metaphors for our naivete and glory.

Sounds of Angels

To believe or not to believe,
that's not a question.
You get sick because you want to.
If the sky has to pour down
the rain, how can you stop your mother
from getting married?
The bus returns to Chinatown from Atlantic City.
The guide stands at the door and says
no one can leave unless each pays an eight-dollar tip.
The old lady from Jersey stands before the seascapes
of Sugimoto, her face inscribed with misfortune.
"Nothing, nothing," she screams, "I see nothing
but blackness." The guard points the way to the impressionist
paintings. "Follow this sign, and you'll see lots of colors and things,"
she says. Far away, birds fly soundlessly across the sky,
transforming it regardless of human perception.
We need an inner light to see what's going on in the ocean.
After the dinner, he suddenly flares up and stalks out
the door. I know you have so much anger toward everything
and you have to fight with every minute of your life. But how long
can that last?
To have faith, but not too much.
To be serious, but not too serious. Things
floating between the conscious and unconscious.
The greatest wisdom is to be like a fool.
For Christmas, I don't have a tree. I sit between the radio and TV
waiting for the songs of "The Little Drummer Boy" or "Rudolf
the Red-Nosed Reindeer." But they never come on.

90

It hurts to go into each word, pulling out
the roots. It causes bleeding, yet necessary,
and we can choose how to take the pain,
with grace or dump it on a shrink or your mother as the Chinese
saying goes: if you can't go to the bathroom, you can always blame it
on the toilet for having no sucking power.
She wanders around Chinatown looking for a place
to learn free English so her daughter can have the apartment
to herself in the morning. Bleeding from unknown wounds,
her body scars upon scars. Once in a while,
she can still laugh, delirious with joy.
That's all that counts. Does it matter who created the world and why?
Tao makes one, one makes two, two makes three,
and out of three leaps life, things boundless . . .
Born on the same date as his mother, he decides
to celebrate their birthdays playing chess for three months.
This is the center of the universe, he says,
stamping the ground under the snowflake
glowing above the crossroads of 59th and 5th.
Around us, the hubbub of buying and selling,
the trees glittering with electric stars.
Too much promise and intimacy from above.
To become like a god or a fairy, one must first learn not to eat.
It's not a secret, but few can give up the pleasure.
The terror of entering the realm of beauty
and its intensity. Are you beautiful? I think so.
After all, we're responsible for our own beauty once we reach forty.

One need not seek or fear and should or should not
children pay back their parents for being born
and brought up in this world? All my Chinese friends
have been spanked on their butts. If they don't hold grudges,
why should I? She's stuck with what she hates most
even though she can choose whatever she wants.
He says something then explains they mean something else.
This can be amusing and infuriating. Not afraid of
making mistakes—what a liberation! Your anxious love is becoming
too much. She waits for the end of the holiday season
so she can go shopping. Between war and Christmas,
which keeps the economy going? Her arrival brought
this year's first snowstorm and since then
I wake up in the puddle of my own sweat every morning.
"Go, go back to Flushing," he roared, slamming the typewriter.
"What else can you do except go home?"
My diary on Aug. 8, 1988 is unreadable, written on my way
to his apartment in Manhattan. Love goes away, not the stains
on the sheet. Remember that time you opened my mouth, and
I haven't been able to stop singing since? The virgin forest is
never barren. Thus out of words, their gestures and silent tunes,
rise the meaning for our existence. What do you do when you lose respect
for your parents? But conscience goes on, and the love for blood
that's thicker than water. He won't let anyone read his palm,
not even my mother. Deep down everyone knows
his or her own fortune. The man from Atlanta insists
that a great Christmas is to be driven in a limousine
to Minawaska for snow booting.

Along the upstate highway, dead deer half-buried in the snow,
their eyes glaring at the passing murderers.
My mother has the power
to make people's hands grow longer or shorter.
"Open, close, open, close," she tells her patients,
moving her hands in front of her breasts. "Imagine you're holding
a ball that is the cosmos."
He speaks a few words in Chinese, and she a few words in English.
But how well they get along!
Sometimes he tries Chinese in his made-up tones and she thinks he's
talking English. When she tries her broken English,
he believes she's just shouting in Chinese.
Still, they have fun. There's so little
conscious lying or games.
Perhaps the best way to love a mother
is to let her be? He's a well-known professor
and she a poor student working part-time in a restaurant.
For ten years, he's been
tracking her down wherever she goes.
For some reason he regards her as his guardian angel.
My guardian angels are my worst enemies.
In December's first snowstorm, the homeless man
is sweeping in front of Veniero's in exchange for food.
"Merry Christmas and Happy New Year!"
he says as I insert my key into the building.
"Same to you! Go home and keep warm."
I shout back, waving through the fluffy snowflakes.
I close the door behind me and freeze, struck by the lightning
of realization. "Wait a minute," I say aloud to myself.

"Does he have a home? Do I have a home?
Do we all really have a home?"
Even Confucius was thrown out
of each country like a stray dog.
Suffering beyond all measure. So far our memories.
And words. Everything we try to convey
is a paraphrase. With gestures and facial
expressions, she wants to tell him that she'll give him
the treatment in his apartment so he won't have to go into
the cold afterward. He thinks she wants to see
his loft on Broadway and find out how rich he is. He gets mad
and gives her only ten bucks after the healing.
It took years to find this Christmas tree, perfect
from all angles. But the nuns wouldn't let it go
until they were told it was dying of old age. If the tree
had a say, would it choose its final destination
in a convent or Rockefeller Center? On the silent night,
my mother kneeling on the floor repairing the cracks
with newspaper strips. My Japanese neighbor (she dyed her
hair blonde) loves cigarettes. Her smoke rises through the floor cracks
all night long. Yesterday on my way
to No Bar, I saw some dog droppings on the unmelted snow
that resembled a flower or three fingers pointing
toward heaven. "Holy shit!" I thought.
"Everything has its own halo and we must always be respectful."
Rocks, plants, and animals always make me laugh.
"Smell it," they order me,
"Smell the ocean in our brains."

The sun and moon flow with impersonal passion,
through clouds darkly. Yes, the light that filters through
the marble walls of the library is a pure light
which is also an inner light.
We've been face to face, my beloved.
Now you're drifting away.
Do you know where you're going?

Flash of Selfish Consciousness

It's easy to do a good deed here and there,
but a different matter to keep it up daily.
For evil has many faces and we must dig
into the bottom of the soul to catch
flashes of selfish consciousness, as Mao urged us
in his *Red Treasure Book.*
It hurts.
"But it's good to be hurt from time to time," says my Chinese doctor,
digging, elbowing, and kneeing into the acupuncture spots
of the body. The body twitches and arches and screams.
With a serene smile on his face, the doctor says,
"Pain awakens the heart, and keeps it in good shape."

When I was seven, I became crazy about *wuxiang dou*—five-spice
beans. My grandma would give me only two or three each time,
five if I was good. So I began to steal coins from under her pillow,
one at a time. When I got fifty-seven fen, I went to the store and
bought a half a kilogram of beans. I took the bag to the kitchen
and poured it onto the greasy table. I put my arms around the
pile. This was all mine. I didn't have to share it with anyone else.
I didn't have to pretend to be a selfless daughter or an elder sister.
I could eat it quickly or slowly, standing or sitting or lying down,
any manner I fancied. I could throw or give it away. I was the mas-
ter of those beans. The kitchen was dark; the sun was shimmering
in the sky of the summer noon; the beans smelled seductive. I
filled my mouth with a handful and chewed until my jaws ached
and numbed. Tears rolled down as I thought life is so good and
wouldn't it be better if no one ever woke up from their nap to
interrupt my happiness.

Happiness is as much anything
an illusion, a hypothesis, or a process
of overcoming a series of pains.
the sensation of feeling uprooted and floating,
or stuck in the present,
unable to move back or forward.

You said too bad women don't give you
a chance. But do I really want a chance?
You placed your hand on my shoulder, your eyes
the look of an animal.

One day I asked,
"Mother, something is wrong with me.
I feel dizzy and nauseuos, my joints hurt
like hell, my face burns and I'm pissing blood."

"Too much sex, my dear daughter."

"Mother, I just got fired from my job, my writing
rejected, and I might lose
my apartment in the summer. What's going on?"

"Sex brings bad luck. How many times do I need to tell you?"

"Mother, my days are now filled with despair,

and my nights are taken over by fever and bouts of sweat.

I can't make friends with women.

Men dump me for lack of tenderness.

Mother, I think I'm going insane."

"This is the last time, daughter:

sex is the root of all sickness and evil deeds.

Look at me. Since your father's death, I got

my health back and my eternal happiness."

Since my father's death, I refuse to belong

to a mother, a nation, or a race. Refusing to bond,

I become nothing. If nothing is a curse,

let it be a curse. Let the sun burst on me

its glaring eye, the night

be full of tickling angels. In the dark,

the dog howls and howls, dragging me

into the abyss of our common origin.

My first evil thought came to me when I was four-and-a-half years old. I was sent from my grandma's place, where I grew up, to a navy kindergarten near my parent's house. I was miserable, but not because I missed my parents. I didn't know them yet. I was miserable because I had to get up at seven in the morning to stand in line for the bathroom. Our bathroom was a mobile one set in the dining room before breakfast time, ten cuspidors lined up neatly in the middle and ten little children sitting there like baby birds in nests. Some moaned with

pinched faces, some cried shamelessly in this deep humilia-
tion, and some stared into space in despair. "Don't even think
of getting off before you make something," our teachers said.
Every few minutes, a kid raised his or her hand and a teacher
ran over to clean up. I said to myself: I can't go to the bath-
room in front of other people, those curious, mocking, indiff-
erent eyes. So I held it in. I held it in until the teachers took
away the mobile toilets and everyone sat down for breakfast,
eating and singing: she can't make it, she can't make it. I
perched alone on the tall cuspidor like a bird stranded in its
own shit, so alone and arrogant, in an atmosphere so unpity-
ing, my head suddenly swollen with an evil wish: May my
body explode and flood all the breakfast bowls with my piss
and shit.

The birth of an infant comes the same way
as a turd, don't you know that?
The game is as good as lost. All you can do
is struggle for a sensation.
Shadows of passersby in the flickering twilight,
the night that cuts on the body—
you know you can't bear it, but you bear it anyway.

So let me tell you how I wrote my first story. It was Spring,
1972. I was a senior in middle school. I had to write journals
to record my daily thoughts and deeds for the class discussion
every Monday. There was a format everybody followed: We
encounter difficulties. We're immediately tempted by evil
thoughts or class enemies. Then Mao's teaching begins to echo
in our ears, helping us to fight off the demons and keep our
pure revolutionary spirit. I was often criticized for writing the

exact same story every week, except for the change of names and places. I argued this was exactly what happened because nothing really happened. They thought I was nuts and told me to add more variety to my content and some spice to the style. So I made up the following story:

> "One morning on my way to school, I passed by a public toilet room. I was reciting a paragraph from Chairman Mao's book so I wasn't paying attention to the road. Someone shouted "hey." I looked up and saw a half-naked man and his penis. (Of course I didn't use the word penis in the journal. I used a more appropriate vocabulary, *shengzhiqi*—reproductive organ. This reproductive organ was pointing high up at the sky and the guy was holding it as if he were holding a red-tassled spear between his legs. My first reaction was to run as fast as I could. Then I remembered our great leader Chairman Mao's teachings: 1) To rebel is to do the right thing; 2) Revolution is not an invitation to a party, but a thunderstorm. So I raised my fists, sang "Cut the Jap ghost's head with a saber"—a most popular song in the seventies—at the top of my voice, and charged at the man standing at the door like an idiot with his pants fallen to his ankles. He turned and ran inside. I heard him trip and make a big splash. I hope he fell into the latrine pit, but I didn't check. It was the men's restroom. Girls shouldn't enter. The end."

That was chosen the best journal of the week.
And that semester, I was awarded the title of "Excellent Red-guard of Chairman Mao" for the first and last time of my life.

He thinks he can be a man

if he quits smoking pot and takes ginseng tea

at two every morning.

Once I had a dream. My mother was my executioner. On our way to the shooting ground, I kept arguing that it wasn't fair. She said, "Do you have anything better to say? You have only two more minutes to live." So I immediately began to count the seconds and tried to grasp the meaning of my life. She tied me to a target tree and fixed my head to the bull's-eye with a thumbtack. She raised the gun and took her time to aim. She took two shots. I dodged. One missed, the other went between my eyes. She came over slowly. I held my breath, pretending I was dead. She pinched my arm. "She's not dead yet, she's not dead," she screamed on and on until I could no longer hold my breath. "I have to breathe," I told myself in the dream. "I have to breathe if I want to live. But if I do, I'll be shot again."

I can hear the sound of silence, the echo

of my inner silence, a silence

which is not a void.

The moment it dawned on me that I didn't want a mother, that's been my goal since I started to walk to get away from her, and all my efforts to please and feel close to her were just a big pretense, a cover-up for my evil instinct. I was crushed, but also liberated. It was also the moment I realized I could become the mother of a child.

I began this poem, determined never to mention the word "Mother" again.

But oh, who can really live without her?

Just stop the fight and let her flow through you.

If you don't have a soul, how can she snatch it?

If you don't have a head, how can she cut it off?

Cease fighting, and you no longer have an enemy.

Day and night devour each other with such despair.

Do not fear to break down, do not.

In order to change, we must all go through a few break-downs of nerves.

I'm turning into a fish. My face is now covered

with scales, rows upon rows.

Evil has so many faces; and love likewise.

Move among the leaves with a gentle touch, please;

for there's a spirit in the grass.

Before us all—

time and unforeseen occurrences.